Skunk Kits

WILD Baby Animals

by Ruth Owen

Consultants:

Suzy Gazlay, M.A.
Recipient, Presidential Award
for Excellence in Science Teaching

Jerry W. Dragoo, Ph.D.
Mephitologist

BEARPORT
PUBLISHING

New York, New York

Credits

Cover, © Tim Fitzharris/Minden Pictures/FLPA; 4–5, © age fotostock/Superstock; 7T, © L. Lee Rue/FLPA; 7B, © Tim Fitzharris/Minden Pictures/FLPA; 8, © Geoffrey Kuchera/ Shutterstock; 9, © Holly Kuchera/Shutterstock; 11T, © Sebastian Kennerknecht/Minden Pictures/FLPA; 11B, © Francois Gohier/Ardea; 12–13, © Robert Lubeck/Animals Animals; 14, © All Canada Photos/Superstock; 15, © All Canada Photos/Superstock; 16B, © All Canada Photos/Superstock; 16–17, © Radius/Superstock; 18, © All Canada Photos/Superstock; 19, © S & D & K Maslowski/FLPA; 20–21, © Frank Lukasseck/Corbis; 22T, © Tim Fitzharris/ Minden Pictures/FLPA; 22C, © Robert Lubeck/Animals Animals; 22B, © Shutterstock; 23T, © Jonathan Larsen/Shutterstock; 23C, © Radius/Superstock; 23B, © All Canada Photos/ Superstock.

Publisher: Kenn Goin
Editorial Director: Adam Siegel
Creative Director: Spencer Brinker
Design: Alix Wood
Photo Researcher: Ruby Tuesday Books Ltd

Library of Congress Cataloging-in-Publication Data

Owen, Ruth, 1967–
  Skunk kits / by Ruth Owen.
     p. cm. — (Wild baby animals)
  Includes bibliographical references and index.
  ISBN-13: 978-1-61772-161-8 (library binding)
  ISBN-10: 1-61772-161-1 (library binding)
  1. Skunks—Infancy—Juvenile literature. I. Title.
  QL737.C248O94 2011
  599.76'8139—dc22
                          2010041248

For more information, write to Bearport Publishing Company, Inc., 101 Fifth Avenue, Suite 6R, New York, New York 10003. Printed in the United States of America in North Mankato, Minnesota.

121510
10810CGC

10 9 8 7 6 5 4 3 2 1

Contents

Meet a skunk family

A mother skunk and her babies peek out from inside a log.

The babies are called **kits**.

The skunk family lives inside the log.

Mother skunk

Kits

5

What is a skunk?

A skunk is a furry animal about the size of a cat.

Skunks have long, bushy tails.

They also have sharp **claws** for digging.

Some skunks are black with white stripes.

Others have spots.

Adult skunk size

Spotted skunk

Striped skunk

Claws

How do skunks stay safe?

Skunks can scare off enemies such as bears!

They lift their tails and spray a stinky liquid at the enemy.

Liquid comes out here

The liquid stings the enemy's eyes.

It smells terrible, too!

Bear cub

Where do skunks live?

Many skunks live in **forests** and on **grasslands**.

Others live in towns and cities.

The yellow parts of this map show where skunks live.

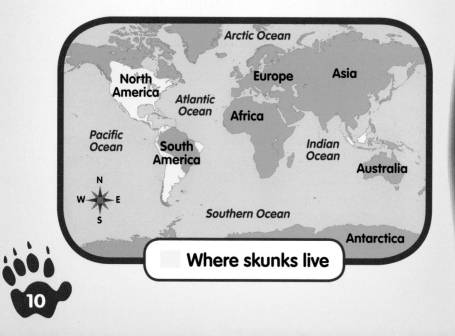

Where skunks live

Skunk homes

Skunks live in homes called **dens**.

Sometimes they dig underground dens.

Sometimes they make their dens inside logs or under houses.

Skunks may even move into empty rabbit or groundhog dens!

Skunk kits

A mother skunk gives birth in a den.

A **litter** may have just two kits.

Some have ten or more!

The mother feeds the kits milk from her body.

Litter of kits

Three-week-old kit

Leaving the den

Kits stay in their den until they are about five weeks old.

Then they go outside with their mother.

The mother skunk protects the kits if an enemy comes close.

Kits

Mother

What do skunks eat?

Skunks eat lots of different foods.

They eat plants, nuts, berries, and eggs.

They use their claws to dig for worms and insects.

Kits watch their mother to learn how to catch insects.

Eggs

The kits leave home

Kits stay with their mother for about three months.

Then they go off on their own.

They know how to find food.

They know how to dig dens.

Now the kits can take care of themselves.

Glossary

claws (KLAWZ) hard, sharp nails on the fingers or toes of an animal

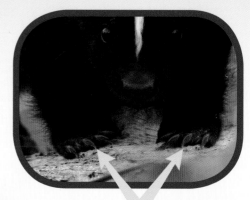

dens (DENZ) homes where wild animals can rest, be safe, and have babies

forests (FOR-ists) places where lots of trees grow

grasslands (GRASS-landz) places with a lot of grass and small plants; only a few trees and bushes grow there

kits (KITS) the babies of some animals, such as skunks and squirrels

litter (LIT-ur) a group of baby animals that are born to the same mother at the same time

Index

Read more

Doudna, Kelly. *It's a Baby Skunk! (Baby Mammals)*. Edina, MN: ABDO (2008).

Markle, Sandra. *Skunks (Animal Prey)*. Minneapolis, MN: Lerner (2007).

Mason, Adrienne. *Skunks*. Toronto: Kids Can Press (2006).

Nichols, Catherine. *Smelly Skunks (Gross-Out Defenses)*. New York: Bearport (2009).

Learn more online

To learn more about skunks, visit **www.bearportpublishing.com/WildBabyAnimals**

About the author

Ruth Owen has been writing children's books for more than ten years. She lives in Cornwall, England, just minutes from the ocean. Ruth loves gardening and caring for her family of llamas.